Allow yourself to be bitten. Loll, linger in this unique collection of serpentine, entrancing poems where "A snake does not mean/ what a snake means." The animal is only terribly hungry, steadily moving through its days of imperception towards clarity. Its hunger will be satisfied even if it must consume itself to survive. Likewise, the speaker has found shedding as a means of survival, a way to be newborn. These poems are close enough to taste, sharp enough to leave marks.

—KWOYA FAGIN MAPLES, author of *Mend*

The potent, lush poems in *Shedding Season* shine with livingness, with life, with "human / experiences salty & bright." Jane Morton skillfully turns the experience of being—of living in a body—over and over in her palm, and each turn reveals something deeper, something more.

—CARRIE FOUNTAIN, author of *Instant Winner*

Shedding Season sparkles with the enchanting essence of myth, prayer, and creation. Morton's vibrant, nimble voice channels the Southern storytelling tradition, rich with visceral language that evokes guts, teeth, and soil "rich to taste." These intimate and tender verses celebrate the beauty found in decay and darkness, exploring the scaly, hidden corners where life emerges and resilience is forged. Through an alchemical journey, *Shedding Season* weaves together an origin story, a love song, and a profound reckoning in an essential collection that captivates and resonates and shimmers with the idiom of Southern life. Morton's poignant voice carries the irresistible music of folk magic, showcasing an exceptional talent for inventive metaphor and lyrical grace.

—ESSY STONE, author of *What It Done to Us*

In spare lines of unwavering clarity, Jane Morton writes on the ruthless, animal persistence of life under inhospitable conditions. Their compressed landscapes and images conjure venom and heat, flies and the sound of rattles from dark corners, and the soft bellies and throats so vulnerable under the surface of it all – violent relationships, knives at the gas station, milk poured in a bowl for a dog after her teeth fall out, and a life in which "We all deserve an apology / We all deserve death. Somehow / We get by with neither. Time passes. Everyone forgets."

–CLEO QIAN, author of *LET'S GO LET'S GO LET'S GO*

"Before I spoke, I was only my body," writes Jane Morton, evoking both the physicality of these poems and the power of this poet's voice—not to transcend, but to excavate and exalt. In lapidary and piercing verse, Morton conjures an ominous, charged atmosphere where craving and revulsion, sudden violence and languorous decay, are inextricable and maybe even interdependent, where "We all do / what we know / even when we hate it." What a thrill to encounter Morton's steely candor, to feel them grip the beloved and "push my fingers in… to feel / the death underneath."

–JOEL BROUWER, author of *Off Message*

SHEDDING

SEASON

SHEDDING SEASON

JANE MORTON

BLACK LAWRENCE PRESS

Black
Lawrence
Press

www.blacklawrence.com

Executive Editor: Diane Goettel
Cover & Book Design: Zoe Norvell

Published 2025 by Black Lawrence Press.
Printed in the United States.

TABLE OF CONTENTS

I.

II.

III.

I.

"Who, surprised and horrified by the fantastic tumult of her drives…
hasn't accused herself of being a monster?"

HÉLÈNE CIXOUS

Snake Lore

Every night I watch the clouds
        knit the sky dark and slowly

unravel. Every time it rains
        I am surprised again.

There are so many signs I refuse
        to make meaning of.

A cardinal comes to my window
        when it goes black, strikes

and strikes the glass.
        The face he meets there bleeds

only as much as he does.
        Used to be I believed

almost everything I saw; I'd watch for signs
        in every drop of blood.

Gory thighs in the morning
        meant good luck. And glory,

glory how you'd lose
        whatever you let in.

Truth was a cottonmouth
        wouldn't kill you

but it'd draw blood and hurt.
        Wouldn't kill you

but it'd make you spit poison.
        Used to be I measured time

in flesh, skin and bone
        pushed up against the wall.

I'd wait and watch your eyes,
        flat dead things

long molted hollow.
        My hands shot birds in free fall.

Now watch: I'll open up
        past the edges, unhinge

from my body like a snake's jaws
        stretch over warmth, bone and blood both.

Here is my open mouth, my wrists
        bound, my belly

blue as milk, warm as a bath.
        Here I am waiting for you

to make it hurt enough,
        make me bite back.

Self Portrait with Grackles

The whole season I am sweating, fall
an illness   blooming. I've noticed

I care less and less
for the shape of me, only

that it is receding.   I say
so many things, all lies. When he touches me

I can feel   the hatred steadying
his hands, keeping them

gentle. It's obvious
I want too much,   to lap from his hands

until I'm satisfied, to suck
on his fingers until they hurt. Asleep,

he says, my breath goes out
in little whines   like a dog

dreaming. This he takes
as a good thing. The body seized ecstatic

in terror. And it's true
there is a voice that says *kill*

and eat, so I know
it is holy, this hunger.   I know

I misunderstand.   When the trees fill out
with grackles, slick black and green

as oil   iridescing, I find
their open throats

so inviting.   I let them
take whatever they can.

Aubade

                    If I close my eyes,
refuse the morning
            the light   falters, becomes
a veil   of warm blood.

                        The stars
haven't left us,   but they hide
            their faces,
bashful or ashamed   of us, saying nothing.
        I stare   through the window,
through my eyelids,

                        willing

the sun to retreat,   or else
        come closer
than ever before,   grow hotter, brighter
        than anyone could stand,
much less us.   I will
        fire, everywhere.   Red blooms

just beneath   my skin, obsessed
        with existing,   being
or waiting to be   touched.
        In the new night

I become   my eyes; I go

where they go.
                It doesn't matter,
my body becoming   wax, slipping
        between your fingers,
your legs,   away
        from itself.   It doesn't matter
that I'm bleeding.

                I've been so tired,
        carrying   myself around.

One Summer He Showed Me Mayflies

a swarm caught

        in the men's room
        one night

at the city pool
legs like loose hair stuck
to tile walls

        a blur of wings
        in the shower

in the morning
my breath still ripe

        with him, hay-
        fragrant

I felt

        my body folded
        tender as a rose

around my hips
the lightest bruises
smaller than I imagined

        and more painful
        than his hands

I almost
couldn't believe

        I earned

all the love I got—

        each drop of spit
        on my tongue

it's not a lie
but it becomes a lie

                in the telling

Dayton, TX

Today he's the saw hanging in the garage:
dusted orange, impotent, mean. A mouthful
of blades and unsure how to use them.
We're sleeping off a rainless summer
at my mother's house, days spent stripping
bark off the cedars, cicadas loud and hot
in our ears, and the air full of water
and dust. Tepid nights where I touched him
and he shivered like something skinned
bare, his flesh burning under mine. We kissed
in the closet, whispered no
like that was the real sin, our fingertips
and throats and tongues more pure than anything
I knew how to beg for. Still there was a time
I worked his violence like a bow, slipping
across horsehair or entrails, attempting beauty.
We sweat ourselves limp and watched:
my stepfather's dog shot straight through
with two bullets, a ring of blood
left around the house, but he didn't die.
When my mother's cow broke through
the fence, gave birth on the empty street,
he followed, running, licking the pavement.

Milk Snake

Who was the first one claimed
there was milk gone missing?

The barn with its carpet of leaves, its cat piss
smell of hay. Sometimes there's a rattle

from a dark corner. Sometimes you can catch
a glimpse of the pale

undulant belly bright against the filth.
And whose idea was it

that the snake not bite but suck
so gently as to almost go unnoticed?

Sometimes a snake does not mean
what a snake means. Milk snake cloaked

in the skin of a viper, pretend-venomous. We still
want to know what wrong you've done.

Promise

Keep me   from speaking.
I don't want to   hurt

any one   of you. But what
does it matter

what I want?   I'm only
the mouth of the animal.

The heart   and the stomach
speak through me.   The throat

its own translation.
And who can blame you

not understanding?
I have nothing   inside me

but hunger.   I knew
it wasn't true   before I said it.

Promise   when the scissors
come out   they'll only cut

what needs   to be cut.
I'll take the pieces

in my hands   and call them
sister.   And take their hands

and call them.   Sister,
I'll eat   your death. All

of them. Hollow   space
carved out of me.   Open mouth

tender, shell   around an egg.
I promise.   Now

I'll always   hold
that space.

Thistle

I swear we didn't touch
last night but still I wake up

reeking of you. The light falling
over the bed so gentle I can only hate it

for a moment. I know you
won't be there when I open my eyes. Still

I open my eyes. What's the use
in saying anything else?

Everyone I love has got bloody
palms, bloody teeth—

I do too. Fingers
pressing wounds

that hurt me but not
me worst of all.

*

*

Worst of all the way thistle clawed
its way to beauty. The way desire broke

my open mouth. That time we cut
the thistle from the highway roadside

my hands and thighs a mess
of shallow marks

we cleaned with spit, my fingers
in your mouth. It didn't hurt

or hurt so sweetly I could nurse it.
Worse the way the heat came

on me after, my blood
an outrage just under my skin.

I didn't even think
to wash my hands.

*

*

Say my hands were caught in the steel
teeth of desire. Say

I was walking on all fours. I was
circling a trail of my own

footprints, my own blood. Say
I didn't know

I was bleeding. When I found you
I was hungry enough

to spit in the dirt and call it
tender. I was hungry enough to taste

my own tongue. When I found you
I didn't know delirium

from fever. I didn't have a name
for what I was.

Drive

I let you talk
       the whole way out

a ragged logic
       unspooling

between us
       dark and thin as a vein

slowly emptying.
       I wanted to be

so quiet I wouldn't be there
       anymore, an hour away

from home and still speeding
       in the same direction.

The road stripped everything
       down to the basics, shadows

uncoiling and receding
       back into the dark, hands

flexing around the wheel,
       around each other.

When there was nothing left
        to say we parked

somewhere between towns
        where the insects

made a new kind of silence
        of their need, legs rubbing

and rubbing, hollow bodies over-
        filling with noise.

There's no one
        out here, you said. *No one*

to see. Your fingers in my mouth
        and my hair.

We thought this was all that mattered.
        All we needed.

Afterwards, I was so hungry
        I can remember the taste

of my own sweat on my wrist
        when I bit down, stinging myself

silent in the dome light. We drove back
        too fast before sunrise

refusing to let the scene become
        beautiful. The radio on

just to remind us how many
        other people are out there.

Overgrowth

Past the overgrowth, dandelion and bull
        thistle. The suffocated blush
            of the wisteria, lank arms and hands

dripping. Past hunger,
        our two crooked marks
            against the night.

We stop walking and sit
        for a while looking at the train,
            hulking sleep we throw stones at

for noise. It's just the kind of hot
        that makes the insects sing
            themselves inaudible, their bodies

thrown against the pavement,
        jewel eyes, stick legs so delicate
            I can't help but pull them off.

It's the kind of hot where nothing moves
        but metal and grease, flesh
            and stone, legs and oiled wings

drawn against each other.
        What is there to say? I can't talk
            when it gets like this.

Mutable dark smearing
        everything unsure. Your face
           an unripe green

bud holding tight. Your face
        a fist. The rocks we throw
           at the train. A fire lit.

Heat Wakes Me

And a citrus smell, warm   hands. He
     wakes me   with hands friction-
warm and imprecise.   Citrus smell of his   hands wakes me
     and it is already happening.

                               Summer runs its last ragged lap
      around us, legs thin
           as chicken legs
and clawed. Little points of blood   too small to bleed.
        Does this count as loss?
How dizzy   the days feel   when it's this hot and still
     dark outside, when the days mount   all languor
and wet   anywhere skin might touch on
             skin, any tender place.
     He wakes me
but I am only ever half-   awake   the warm green
          sea-sick hour
    before the sun.   His hands rough, turning red
the morning   where I'll vacate, half
     myself and empty   but for him.
              I'm telling you

it's so hot my eyelids   are slick, my eyes
     burn and I can't see you
through it. It's too hot   to breathe
     and I can't tell you anything about it.

II.

"I'd rather starve death than myself."

DOROTHY ALLISON

Dogwood

Trim the mistletoe from the dogwood.
How'd that ugliness convince us

it was romance? How'd we make
a home when all we had

we'd stolen? Come lie down
on the floor again. Remember

how we'd lie and sleep there
slick and still as copperheads?

Lie here too long
and you'll wake with a roach in your hand.

Plenty of dust
in your belly. Plenty of dirt

in your hair. Back then we let ourselves
dry out in full sun. We knew

what we were doing.
Remember how I begged

to dim the lights
for just a moment? I took your hands

and put them on my neck.
Back then we kept

a jar of sugar out for ants.
Watched them come in rivers, fill

the white with motion.
A feral altar. All those ants

spread through whatever
sweetness we had, indiscriminate.

Ungrateful children, we laughed
and killed them. We all do

what we know
even when we hate it.

We know to eat
the fat and chew the bones

for when we've got none.
We know how meanness lives

its own life in the meat and marrow.
A strand of blood

in the eyeball, a bit of yellow.
A rope of blood

spit through teeth.
We know these things

happen all the time.
Like when our rooster goes

and pecks our hens
to pieces. Panic

of feathers in the air.
They keep on laying eggs.

There Are So Many Flies in the Kitchen

My eyes are hot with them,
        their noise,   filthy white
noise, trembling,
                irresistible weight.

                        They trap me
thinking
        of the opossum   I saw vibrating
with flies just outside the house, down
        the driveway.   I approached
eagerly, wanting to touch
        the shiny black,   incessant—

                        I still
                want it.

I cover my ears with my hands,
        my head   with a blanket,
leave all the lights on and wait
        for quiet to come.   It doesn't.
Your fingertips move
        like flies on my face.
I'm stuck, I tell you,   *behind*
        the blinds.   I can see the light
just outside, the blinds' broken
                invitation   to slip through.

When I slip through, suddenly
          it's so hard   to say what is good,
what is real,   what is not.

Snake Lore

A flock of open throats spills
noise like sun over the dirt
out back, meaning a snake is near.
Each body a quiver,
scaled feet all claws. Each point
a portent scabbing over. Tell me
again what it means
to keep a snake in the home,
about the girl who let the snake
in her back yard drink
from her, who held the snake
in her lap like an infant, her chest
bent to him. How sickly
she was and pale and her eyes
bloodless yellow and how cold.
Tell me again
how they found the snake
behind her house
and cut his head off
with the garden hoe and draped
the body over the fence.
How when they went to check
on the girl in her bed,
always in her bed until late
in the morning she was dead too,
her blue neck bent and strangled.

You can hear the snake's
rattle, quiet underneath
the birds' bloody murder cries
if you listen close. You can hear
the snake's cold belly
winding in the dust. That snake
ate all our chickens' eggs
and then ate all our chickens too.
Tell me again
how we are watched over, all
of us, by a jealous god.
How he knows each hair
on our pretty heads, each scale
on our twisting backs.

Cottonmouth

When the dog comes home
snakebit, soaked through the coat

with bad water, my mother knows
we'll find the snake

flung limp in the dirt, holes
bright in the belly.

Some say the flesh of the snake
will cure its bite. We think

we know better. Know to bite harder
than you're bit, and then let go.

Once the swelling goes down,
the dog's teeth are soon to fall out.

When they do, we'll pour
a little milk in her bowl.

Development

The city grows
too fast, sends deer out

into the streets, hulking
miracles our greed

sweat out. Someone I knew
took his crossbow on a drive

one night in the middle
of a party at his dad's house

and strung one up
by her hind legs

in the garage, a bucket
filling up below her

cut throat. We were
kids, but didn't know it.

There were so many
he said, it's a shame

not to eat
what you're given.

Noon with Shotgun and Cedars

A bruise weeps warmth
over my shoulder.   Kickback

strong enough it knocked me down
the first time,   the grass slick

and itchy on my thighs. We're out
past the snake tree,
past the creek.   The cedars

tall, waving
their shredded bark   goodbye.
We're shooting   nothing. Trusting

no one else   could end
up here besides us.

Refrain

i.

Midday the sky strains over us
        continuous white
as a sheet stretched
        over a mattress.
It's almost safe,
        almost sacred,
something you could have
        been born on.

We forget for a moment
        we are in
the most terrible place:
        the light cruel, the animals
all murdered, waiting
        at the side of the road,
the sun ravaging
        the flies ravaging them.
We spit every time
        we pass another one.
We don't belong here.
        Tell me
we don't belong here.

ii.

Midday the sky is threadbare
fabric we huddle under, colorless
light coming through in patches.
I look at you to make the noise stop,
to make the itching stop, to make
me lie down. I need you watching me,
your eyes a green wet fester I want
to push my fingers into, to feel
the death underneath.

iii.

Midday the sky is hollow, broken
          open, eggshell white and damp.
I touch you like a wasp nest, like a needle
          coming down again and again.
I am blue ink, a gangrene
          you can't shake off.
Kick me:
          I will come back.
You know this.

Crown of thorns, crown of flies
          circling your head.
Hollow, your eyes
          drink up all the light. Come
lie down. Come
          kiss the sweat off my neck.
Kiss the sun away.
          Make it night again.

Overnight

Morning, and I am still not home.
        Your house a slow-healing hurt. My face
            a blue mirror to look through.

Morning, and the dark is cut with a dull blade
        of light I covet, how it holds the dust without
            reciprocation, fingernail and carapace alike

in the after, no questions asked. And how to fall
        like that—how to let go. What grip I have
            already bruising.

We are not our bodies,
        but we hurt when they do,
            we hunger. Tongues thick

as windowpane. And what light
        lets in. What glass can't staunch.
            What glare

an illusion of blindness. Morning,
        and we cannot pretend
            not to see anymore.

Thighs slick as roach, and your mouth
    a nightmare opening,
        a toothy constellation. Morning,

and a crescent moon bruise twists,
    harvest yellow. Bad blood, old
        blood the hardest to cast off.

Self Portrait in the Mirror

So small I cut myself
        into sections: jaw & neck,

cunt & thigh. My mouth
        red as a match end.

I only want to see
        what we've anointed,

the parts still wet and warm as tongue.
        Shut my eyes

to all that isn't glossy, slick as spit
        I'd take from your mouth

into mine. Slow
        how a bruise blooms. Slow

how the dark comes on at first
        without warning

before it leaves you blindfolded, tied
        to the bed. And leaves you

to come up with an answer. What
        you're scared of. The hushed creek, the fat

hum insect legs find against each other.
     And light, thin as snakeskin

veined and broken in the molt.
     What wrath: my eyes

can't help but let
     the light break in.

What wrath: my body
     rushes back to meet itself.

Red Film

We haven't talked in a week
when you pull up, haggard nonchalance
and gas station coffee.
You can't be trusted, you half-joke,
to drive us. I don't ask where we're going.
I've stopped pretending
this will be the last time. I sit back
and watch your hands move
languid on the wheel, the gear shift,
my skirt. A shock of flowers
lies in the backseat, forgotten pink
faces a crumpled fist. My fear
a Venus flytrap, dormant
until touched, then venom, gradual
decay. You still think
I'm a good girl and yours no less.
The truth is I have already left
the morning, white as cataracts, blue
underneath. The sun halfway
up the window and glaring,
a thousand eyes. When you kiss me
I bite down too hard. Red film
on my teeth when I laugh. I see you
notice. Suck the blood off.

Folding Knife

We stop at a gas station and I buy
      a six pack, chips, and toothbrushes
you open with your folding knife,
      laughing. I take it,
press my tongue to the blade, trying
      to show you how okay I am
with everything that's happening.
      I fumble folding the knife shut
and you snatch it back.
      You're doing it wrong, you say, always
concerned how I might hurt
      myself. I keep trying to brush off
the danger. Doing it wrong. Even now,
      I'm still doing it wrong.

Shedding Season

Before bees caught in my hands,
     shaking. Before my mouth

filled with honey. Before the cottonwoods shed
     and made spring winter.

Woolly seed all in the air like snow. No way
     of knowing it would hurt me

just to breathe it. My chest mottled the same red
     as my hands, breaking hard

bewildered fruit just for the sting. Bitter juice
     hot as batteries, a fat lip.

Before you met me, I was my own
     fever. My own bite bruising.

And how could I have known how
     heat breaks. How to show

teeth without the blood. Stubborn
     smudge on a mirror, no way

of knowing how you'd haunt
     what I see there.

When the trees shed it's already over:
        sexed in secret, a closed bud.

Before I spoke, I was only my body.
        All blooming rash, all asthma

evidence kept flesh-deep. Before you named me,
        I was so many things.

Before your mouth, a line
        of ants drawn down my back.

Solstice

How long until the fruit begins to rot?
The parts we've wasted lie
around the kitchen—over-soft
strawberries, pomegranate seeds we forgot
to eat, tomatoes wet and veined as hearts
quartered on the counter, a fly in your hair.
My mouth is full of red.
The walls are full of flies you'd only know
if you listened right.

The heat never breaks this time
of year but we don't know that yet.
We sit out on the front steps
and watch the sky burn to soot,
sweat beading my forehead
a crown. We wait for a sign
we should or shouldn't quit; a sparrow
or a crow, something feathered,
unfettered or fallen.

When the light goes,
all we have to watch are flies,

unafraid or careless, hardly
moving. We could go on
forever like this. Our lives unspooling
before us. We won't die
all at once, but piece by piece—an ache
creeps in marrow-deep.
It takes a while even to notice.
The night almost at the end of its rope.

Split Portrait

i.

Sometimes there are two
      of us. Sometimes we are both

in the room. I am sitting still as a knife
      and she is spinning

somewhere above me. A photograph
      poked full of holes and hanging

from a string. A makeshift lure
      I bite. Every time there is blood

in the air. Every time the light
      bleeds through differently.

ii.

In the dark I drop my shape,
      my knife. Clothes tossed

on the floor. A fairy circle
      around the bed, attempted

protection. I'm always under
        the covers when I undress.

I always wait until morning
        to tidy up.

iii.

Greedy for giving, I spill
        across the bed, a wound

old as hunger, festering.
        Often, nausea. Often,

damp sheets in the morning.
        I am not a woman, but god

doesn't care. Pits me red, candy
        pulp on the tile. The bathtub,

the morning their own violence. I hold
        my own head underwater.

iv.

Every time I find another
        way home.

I find another name to call
        myself. I find

a familiar in a window. I smile
　　at my reflection.

Aubade with Cow Tongue and Wisteria

Morning unbruises the sky
in slow motion, dark running
to yellow.   I realize
I could let the day slip
from us like a robe, damp and heavy

and empty.   And then I've done it. Yes
there's vodka in the orange juice.
There's wind in the curtains, taut
as a belly.   I'm far
from famished. He told me once
he saw the cow's tongue hanging
to dry in the kitchen. Dark and slack
as the stirring in his gut. I could never

understand. The wisteria's grown
so fast this year it matches the sky
in its blooming. Every day
breaking out overhead.   He says
you might as well not be here
if you're not coming back. And I know

I'm not.   I'm already off, starting over
in a new place—I just have to
find it. Watching myself
make all the wrong steps. Thinking

any moment I could come out.
Take my hand   and make me
pay   for every minute of our time.

Cardinal

If a cardinal haunted me,
little flame, little heart beating
against the window
at my father's gutted house,
what then?

It doesn't matter now. Come pull
the thin bandage
of my dress from my body.
Wipe the black from my eyes.

What is beauty when you would
lick my bones clean
as a dinner plate? You said
I see your thighs and I have to
bite down. There is no question. My spit
pours over.

And aren't birds always
a promise? Even the buzzards
a slim auguring
flock, circling to show death
where to land. Promising death
will find its way into the ground.

And why shouldn't I? Why
shouldn't I bite
the hand in my mouth?

It's true once I taste the salt
on your skin I won't stop but drink
you dry and fill you with my own spit.

What else can I do to banish hunger,
that uninvited guest, so violent as it grows
more comfortable, taking first what I offer,
then demanding more—all the fat,
all the metal I can muster?

What else can I do but eat
as the moths would eat, holes
in everything I've taken care to fold so nicely
before hiding in its drawer?

"…and I saw a great many bones on the floor of the valley, bones that were very dry.

He asked me, 'Can these bones live?'"

EZEKIEL 37

When They Cut Your Throat

When they cut your throat
was that where I began? A wound

dragged across continents, a cravat
to cover up. I always wanted

to untie the cloth. When you died
I asked if I could

take a bone and keep it.
What am I saying? I don't even remember

your face. I never got to see
the scar. A brittle inheritance,

a name changed to suit
a new home, known to be hostile.

Dark eyes and a jawbone
harder than steel toes, a smile

that is always something else.
Have we always been a family

dismembered? We who don't know our own
faces, but know when to burrow,

when to sting? I'm saying
I always keep my throat

covered up. I always keep my eyes
on my hands.

My hands in fists. I always believed
in the myths, what was hidden

around the old house. A severed toe
in the attic, a box of hair.

All the parts of us
we'd parted with. I thought

if I could find them
I could start again.

Self Portraits in Retrospect

It hasn't been a good year, but it's almost over now, the me who lived it
        almost dead, tossing and turning under white sheets.
I'm packing up the house. I'm taking everything:
        all the jewelry, all the knives, the child I found, just born,
        black around the neck.
I'll raise her as my own. Nurse her
        with tap water, my body
        not yet giving milk.
If she cries, I'll put her to bed, light a cigarette,
        crawl in with her, cradle her.
And if the old me drops by, childless, knife-handed, and demands
        her fair share, I'll swear I never knew her.
Maybe she'll weep. And I'll weep with her, my new life
        curled between us.
I'll invite all the other mes: *crawl in, cry*. We all deserve an apology.
        We all deserve death. Somehow
we get by with neither. Time passes. Everyone forgets.

Drought

There was the time I drove the car into the creek,
     and then the time I was the creek
         and almost drowned.

There was a year that turned the creek to stone.
     It wound its way through woods
         that aren't quite woods.

Trees too pale and nervous to be trees
     and grass that reached up
         taller than I was.

In February I was getting better.
     The year began as gentle as a specter.
         The air as clear and terrible as sight.

The doctor's hands were small
     and blue; they flitted.
         Death chewed steady

on my wrists, my hips. He touched
     my hair and eyelids, tongue
         and veins. I sucked

on stones and clawed
     the dirt beneath them. Fingernails
         dark crescent fertile moons.

I chewed them off, chewed steady
        through the morning. Mayfly nymphs
                disrupted from their death-sleep.

Dreams of swarm, of flight, of body heat.
        I held the doctor's hand; he touched
            my shoulder.

Watched my blood crawl slow into the summer.
        More promises we knew
            I couldn't keep.

I'd give myself up for another, hungrier.
        I've traded self for self
                yet I'm still me.

I thought I couldn't live
        like this; I go on living.

Distance

I never want to talk about the past
until it ripens. Until time has softened
every detail to rot.
I never want to tell you how it felt
what we were doing. Unnamed and naked
down to the bone. I'll only say
what I wanted
you to say. Make my body
ours; close my mouth
to any contradiction.
If I could, I would tell the truth
about us: the beds I burned
to get here. The ash I ate.
I'd retrace every step: the courthouse,
the needle, the summer
that sweated me through fall.
Instead I'll ask about the likelihood
of rebirth, if a new body can be stripped
of old blood. I'll name us
the answer. The truth is
I can only stand to look back
from a distance like a stranger, to watch us
fall how evening falls,
so graceful, so inevitable you might forget
to be afraid of the dark.
The truth is I have always been the stranger:

no roots of my own. I keep taking
what doesn't belong to me.
I never let go.

Snake Lore

I was raised to know the devil
when I see him. His red mouth loose

and rage-drunk, shouting, laughing.
He plays like he's not angry, not

at me. Tonight he finds
his way into my bedroom.

His skin as wet as snakeskin
up against me. Sweet venom

like turpentine he breathes. Says
aren't we having fun?

But he's not asking. His eyes flat
yellow pennies, cheap

metal things. There's no one here
to eat the fruit besides me.

The cherry of his cigarette
exhausting. The stars watch

but they don't watch over me.
When I bite, there's blood, the same

as when he bites me.
I was raised to know the devil

when I see him. The night is lonely,
it won't let me sleep.

Self Portrait with Feathers

The night hangs open: a dark wet mouth where I languish.
        Or a nest, thorny halo full of need: empty
                bellies, open throats.

There are so many just like me, waiting it out.
        Stars woven thick as barbed wire around us.

I'm saying I've been helpless, unfed. Hollow-boned
        and clumsy, asking anyone to pick me up.

I have fallen. Slipped from myself like a skin
        pulled from boiled milk.

My feathers still wet, and my smell, so wrong
        not even a mother could recognize it.

All that strange skin, the unseen
        touches. Think of the confusion

on both sides, the imminent hunger.
        How anyone could possibly stand it.

Tiktaalik

1.

Fish-bellied mother surviving,
        slit-bellied fish we've fed from,
                transubstantiated from the shallows-

scum detritus of our past,
        we cannot look you in the eye.
                We cannot tell you where

we have been since we left.
        We cannot say much
                for progress or personhood,

a cannibal act subsumed
        in time's vagaries; we know
                only what we have

become: the eaters of flesh.
        We are famished.
                We swallow whole all things

we don't know, a slow digestion
        of the self. We are performing
                ourselves. Mother,

come up from the water.

      Mother, half-drowned,

            half-alive between our teeth.

2.

if only a handful
of teeth if only a bone
fragment if the absences
say more than her body still
we can say snakelike
we can say a large skull
a large jaw expanding
in the water we can say predation
& fear the first human
experiences salty & bright
where she swam
shallow & warm if she bore
young if she was made to
bleed if she mothered
if she fed them
her own flesh if she lost
herself piece by piece
until she was only backbone
only teeth and eventually
even the teeth were lost
before we found her &
said that she was nearly whole

Chorus, Legs on Legs

There was a season
            of spit
and cigarettes
            on the street
I found
            all the time

only half-
            used up
but dead

            everyone was
dying

            I spent

whole days outside
            perched on the roof
crouched there

            the mosquitos
forming

            a vigil

I made
my family
I devoured

them

squandered

parts of me too
the skin I sloughed
my breath

haunted

a chorus of legs on legs
humming
all the insects

a tangled crown

a hundred drops
          of my blood   suspended
enough to make you
          sick
to gag

          a song
                                         I swore
I'd sing

for the last time—
                                         I'd claw my way out

& be new.

Acknowledgments

Many thanks to the publications in which many of these poems first appeared, including the following:

"Snake Lore I" in *Passages North*
"Self Portrait with Grackles" in *Gulf Coast* as "Hunger"
"Aubade" "One Summer He Showed Me Mayflies" and "Shedding Season" in *The Rupture*
"Milk Snake" in *Sugar House Review*
"Promise" in *West Branch*
"Thistle" and "There Are So Many Flies in the Kitchen" in *Hunger Mountain*
"Drive" and "Refrain" in *New South*
"Overgrowth" in *Cutbank*
"Dogwood" in *Third Coast*
"Dayton, TX" in *Yemassee Journal*
"Snake Lore II" in *Boulevard*
"Cottonmouth" and "Solstice" in *Chicago Quarterly Review*
"Development" in *Quarterly West*
"Self Portrait in the Mirror" in *Ninth Letter*
"Overnight" in *Poetry Northwest*
"Split Portrait" in *BOOTH*
"Aubade with Cow Tongue and Wisteria" in *The Journal*
"Snake Lore III" in *The Lilac Issue* of *Fairy Tale Review*
"Drought" in *Redivider*
"Self Portraits in Retrospect" in *Muzzle Magazine*
"Distance" in *Frontier Poetry*

"Self Portrait with Feathers" in *Meridian*
"Tiktaalik" in *The Offing*
"Chorus, Legs on Legs" in *Poet Lore*

Some of the poems included in this collection were also published, sometimes as earlier versions or under different titles, in the Black River Chapbook Competition-winning chapbook *Snake Lore* (Black Lawrence Press).

I owe so many thanks to Diane Goettel and everyone at Black Lawrence Press for all the time and attention you've given to this book – I couldn't have asked for better people to work with.

Finally, I have endless gratitude for my friends, family, and teachers, and especially for those of you who have been all of these things for me at one time or another. Grey Wolfe, my first reader and partner in everything, thank you for all that you are and all that you've given me along the way.

JANE MORTON is the author of *Shedding Season* and *Snake Lore*, both published by Black Lawrence Press. Their poems have also been published individually in journals including *Gulf Coast*, *West Branch*, *Boulevard*, *Passages North*, and *Ninth Letter*. They hold an MFA from the University of Alabama, where they were Online Editor for *Black Warrior Review*. They are an Assistant Professor at Grand Valley State University, where they teach poetry and creative writing.